Skull of the Vampire

DELUXE ADVENTURE MODULE

The Lord Vandrac Chronicles VI

An Adventure Module for 1 Player
For the Hammer + Cross RPG
Designed by Noah Patterson

Hammer Cross

Skull of the Vampire
The Lord VanDrac Chronicles V.1
Copyright © 2020 Noah Patterson
ISBN: 9798687735803

Find us on DriveThru RPG
Or at MicroRPG.weebly.com

Cover Artwork by Dean Spencer Art

Abbey Map art by Patrick E. Pullen

Rat King Illustration used under Creative
Commons

Section 6.1 art by Jose Cardona

STOP!

DON'T BUY THIS BOOK!
At least, not yet.

The basic rules for the Micro Chapbook RPG system and Hammer + Cross found in this book can be downloaded for FREE through DriveThruRPG.com in the Manor of Blood book. Give the system a try before you buy.

With that in mind, this Deluxe Adventure Module includes everything you need to play the game.

You don't need any other book to experience the game!

Contents

Section 1.0

What is Skull of the Vampire?

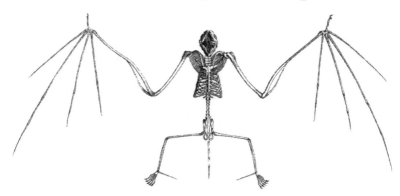

Skull of the Vampire is an adventure module for the Hammer + Cross Roleplaying game system and is the first volume in the Lord VanDrac Chronicles story arc. Each volume in the 5 book series stands on its own, but all connect to create a greater campaign. Therefore, this adventure can be played on its own or as part of the larger VanDrac story arc.

This book includes the basic rules to allow you to play the game. However, the Hammer + Cross core rulebook will go into greater detail on all elements of the game. Hammer + Cross uses the Micro Chapbook RPG system and, therefore, this book can be combined with any other books or genres in the same system.

For those new to the system, Micro Chapbook RPG is an ultra rules-light fantasy-based game designed specifically for the solitaire gamer in mind--but is adaptable for co-op play as well as traditional Game Master driven gameplay.

Hammer + Cross is a Gothic Horror rendition of the traditionally fantasy-based game system. In Hammer + Cross, you take on the role of vampire and monster hunters in an alternate version of late 1800s Victorian Europe where evil abounds. The game is strongly influenced by the Hammer Horror films of the 60s and 70s.

Section 2.0

What Do You Need?

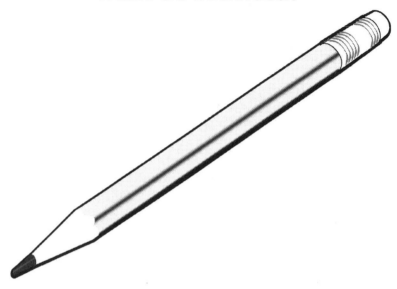

To play this adventure you will need:

- A Pencil and Eraser
- A Sheet of Graph Paper
- A Character Sheet
- 2 Six-Sided Dice
- This Adventure Book
- The Hammer + Cross Core Rulebook (Optional).

Section 3.0

Rules Basics

Hammer + Cross is an ultra-simple roleplaying game that can be played solo (or with a traditional GM if you so wish). In the next few pages, you will find the basic rules for the game system:

What You Need: 2 six-sided dice, graph paper, notepaper/character sheet, a pencil w/eraser, Scenario Maps/Sticker, this chapbook.

Rolling: During play, you always roll 1D6, trying to score equal to or lower than your stat score. If you are proficient, roll 2 dice and take the better result of the 2. 1 always succeeds. 6 always fails. (NOTE: When you see 1D3 it means you roll a die and half the result rounding up.)

Characters: To create a character, do the following:
1. **STATS:** You have 4 statistics. **ST**rength, **DE**xterity, **WI**ts, **CH**arisma. You have 7 points to assign between them as you see fit (9 for an easier game). No stat can have a score lower than 1 or higher than 4 at this point.
2. **CLASS:** Choose a class. There are 4 to choose from. Each one will make you proficient in one area.
   a. **Soldier:** Proficient in ST
   b. **Hunter:** Proficient in DE
   c. **Nurse/Doctor:** Proficient in WI
   d. **Priest/Nun:** Proficient in CH
3. **ORDER:** Choose an Order to join. Your Order grants you a +1 bonus to one stat.

a. **Order of the Hammer:** +1 ST
b. **Order of the Dagger:** +1 DE
c. **Order of the Cross:** +1 WI
d. **Order of the Sun:** +1 CH

4. **HEALTH, WILL, & FAITH:** Your health is your ST+DE+20. Your will is your WI+CH+20. Your Faith is your Wits + 20 (+ 25 if you're a Priest/Nun).

Weapons: Roll 2D6 to determine your money. You may buy equipment now. Weapons have a damage rating and a cost in pounds (£). Below are some basic starter weapons, both ranged and melee. You may have 2 melee and 1 ranged at any given time. You may buy these and others in town as well.

Melee Weapons			Ranged Weapons		
Dagger	1	1g	Holy Cross	1	2g
Wooden Stake	1D3	2g	Holy Water Sprayer	1D3	3g
Hammer	1D3+1	3g	Rusty Revolver	1D3+1	5g
Cane Sword	1D6	4g	Blessed Long Whip	1D6	6g
Silver Sword	1D6+1	5g	Crossbow	1D6+1	7g

Armor and Items: Armor grants the wearer a boost to their health, will, or both. Other items such and food and potions can be used to restore lost health and will. On the next page are some basic starter items and armors. You may buy these and others in town as well.

Armor			Items		
Shield	+3H	1£	(2) Bread Crust	1D3 H	1£
Top Hat	+3W	1£	(3) Wine	1D3 W	1£
Black Cloak	+6H	2£	(4) Steak Meal	1D6 H	2£
Chainmail	+6W	2£	(5) Holy Water	1D6 W	2£
Blessed Robes	+6HW	3£	(6) Miracle	FULL HW	6£

Generating Rooms: Begin by choosing a random square on the graph paper and generating the first room. To generate a room, roll 2D6. The number rolled in the number of squares in the room. These can be drawn in any way, shape, or form so long as they are orthogonally connected. Next, roll 1D3 (1D6 divided by 2 rounded up). This is the number of NEW doors in the room (not including the door you just came through). Draw small rectangles to represent the doors along any single square's edge to designate an exit.

Room Type: Each newly generated room has a type. Roll 1D6 on the scenario Room Chart to determine the type. Note this in the room with the type's letter code as listed on the chart.

Doorways: Next, you will choose one door to move through into the next room. Roll 1D6 to determine the door type. After moving, generate the new room. (This chart is also provided in each scenario).

(5–6)	Unlocked	Move through freely.
(4)	Stuck	Must make a ST check to get through. Lose 1 WILL to reroll and try again.
(3)	Locked	Must make a WI check to get through. Lose 1 WILL to reroll and try again.
(1–2)	Trapped	Must make a WI check to disarm and move. If you fail, take 1D3 damage but still move through.

Monsters: After Entering any room. Roll to generate the monsters in the room. Roll once for the monster type (on the scenario Monster

Chart) and a second time for the number of that monster. Each monster has a Max number of that type that can appear in a room, a Health Damage, a Will Damage, and a Life Force. **Vampires** also have two additional special stats:

- **Bloodletting (BL):** Each time the player rolls a 6 during a melee attack (an instant failure), the vampire bites them and drinks their blood. The BL is how much LF it regains.
- **Power (P):** This is the mental strength of the vampire. It is the amount of faith the player will lose if they fail during the Faith check.

Fighting: To fight the monsters in your room, follow these steps in order:

1. **Bravery:** Make a CH check. If you pass, gain 1 Will. If you fail, you lose Will according to the monster's W DMG. If your Will is ever 0, all rolls take a +1 modifier. (A roll of 1 STILL always succeeds)
2. **Ranged Attack:** IF the room is 4 squares or larger you may make a ranged attack. Roll a DE check. If you succeed, apply weapon damage to the monster's LF.

3. **Melee Attack:** You MUST now make a melee attack using a ST check. If you succeed, apply the weapon's damage to the monster's LF. If you fail, roll the H DMG for one monster and apply it to your health. If you have a second melee weapon equipped, attack again.
4. **Repeat:** Repeat this entire process until either you die or you've killed all the monsters in the room. Run away with a successful CH roll.

Faith Check: After battle, if the player was bitten by a vampire during combat, that player makes a WI check. If the player fails, they lose Faith in the amount of the vampire's power. The player may spend 1 Willpower to reroll this check. If Faith reaches 0, the character dies and becomes a vampire.

Search: After battle roll 1D6. If you get 1 through 5 you earn that much money. If you roll a six, roll on the Items table included in the scenario (or the one here in this section. The number to the left of each item is the search roll number). If you roll a 1 on the items chart you find nothing.

The Boss: The boss of the dungeon will not appear until you've encountered all the other monsters in the scenario at least once. Additionally, it will only appear in specific room types as outlined in each scenario. If you roll the boss when it can't appear, reroll. Once the boss is defeated, the game ends.

Alternate Boss Rule: (for potentially quicker games) Keep track of each monster you kill during the dungeon. After each battle is won, roll 2D6. If the roll is LOWER than the number of monsters killed during the dungeon, the boss can now have a chance of appearing. The boss will only appear in specific areas, as designated by the scenario rules. If you roll the boss when it can't appear, reroll.

Leveling Up: In between games you may spend 100 gold to add +1 to one stat (or 50 for an easier game). No stat can be higher than 5. For an easier game, simply level up whenever you defeat a boss. You may also buy new equipment. You may only have 2 melee and 1 ranged weapon at a time.

Section 4.0

Adventure Background

The air is bitter cold as you step outside into the bustling city of London. You're used to the wet October weather, but are unprepared for the chill that has unexpectedly set in. Just the day before, the streets of London were warm with the autumn sun beating down on the cobblestone drives. Overnight, things have taken a cold turn. The smoke and steam of the city churns out into the grey sky. Standing in front of The Order's private headquarters--a skinny building sandwiched in between two other identical ones like it--you pull your overcoat tighter around your body as the rain begins to pitter down from above.

The rattle of wooden wheels and horses hooves draws your attention as your ride turns the corner and stops in front of you. Climbing aboard your chartered carriage, you begin the couple hours journey from the city to the Cotswold.

Somehow, it feels even colder inside the carriage and you wish you had a blanket to wrap over your legs. Still, you settle in. This is a prime opportunity. It is a rarity to have supernatural occurrences so close to home. Usually, you are forced to travel days by train, boat, carriage, and even foot to your destination--most often found in the deep and forgotten areas of eastern Europe.

This, however, is close to home. Somehow, that doesn't comfort you at all. Could it be possible that evil is gaining a foothold in England? Is there a monster of ancient folklore right on your doorstep? There is only one way to find out.

Before you know it, you are shaken awake by the carriage stopping. You blink your eyes, realizing you've fallen asleep. Pulling back the shade, you peer out to see heavy mists sweeping over the green country. Trees of orange and yellow add a splash of color despite the dim light and rainfall.

"We're here," the driver yells, slapping the side of the carriage without even bothering to get down and open the door for you. Helping yourself, you open the door and adjust your hat before stepping out. Standing before you like a monolith of a medieval time is the high walls of a convent. Isolated from any specific village, the grey stone walls appear to loom ominously over you. Could something evil truly have taken hold in a place of such holiness?

Steeling yourself, you walk forward up the path, crossing a short stone bridge over a swelling creek. Making a fist, you knock on the large wooden door. Almost instantly, it cracks open and an elderly nun's face pops out. "You're expected," she shoots off without so much as a hello, stepping aside to allow you admittance.

Once inside, she slams the huge door with surprising ease. Latching the huge bar back over it she gives a stiff nod to follow. You expect her to lead you to the abbey at the center of the convent's complex, but she doesn't. Instead, you head to the dormitory. You're glad to be out of the rain, but the chill of the old building is almost too much. Climbing a curved stone staircase, you come to a small room with a makeshift office. Inside is the Mother Superior.

The Mother's Light Convent is a large, yet seemingly humble, religious campus in the remote English countryside. With a high wall to keep prying eyes out, and to keep the sisters within in good faith, the place seems like a sanctuary of hope and goodwill. Who could ever suspect evil to lurk there?

Well, in this case, the Mother Superior who oversees the place does. While outsiders are hardly ever allowed past its high walls, they have made an exception for you. You hardly saw a single nun on your way in beside the one who greeted you and the Mother Superior. You assume all the women are in their rooms. Is it because this visitor has come OR were they already confined to quarters earlier due to . . . something else. "You'll have to forgive Sister Agatha," the Mother Superior notes, "she is strained just like the rest of us. The situation is dire." She begins to explain how the abbey has been temporarily abandoned. All activities, rites, and services have been forced into the outer buildings.

You may ask the following questions of the Headmistress:

- **Why was the abbey abandoned:** She tells you that is all started when some of the girls began hearing whispers at night. Rumors of a spirit haunting the building started spreading like wildfire through the convent. At first, the Mother Superior had discounted such nonsense. However, when the holy water suddenly transformed into blood, she grew concerned. Then, when the infestation began she had no choice but to move everyone out.

- **If you ask about the infestation:** She informs you that rats started appearing everywhere in the building. Huge and vile things. One bit a Postulant which landed her in the infirmary of the large outbuildings. Since then, the rats only came in hordes. Some writhed in huge twisted knots as if a single mind controlled the mass.
- **If you ask why she called an Order focused on supernatural investigations rather than someone to remove the vermin:** She claims to have already tried multiple other routes to rid their convent of this curse. However, as a woman of God she also believed in the devil, "and the devil is here with us now," she whispers across her desk.
- **If you ask about the Postulant who was bitten:** She offers to take you to the infirmary to see the suffering young girl. You agree.

Section 4.1

The Infirmary

As you walk the length of the dormitory building toward the infirmary, you can't help but note the deathly quiet that hangs in the air. Even the rain from outside doesn't seem to penetrate the stone walls. The only sound is your footsteps and the occasional whisper of prayer from behind doors you pass.

Stepping through a large archway, you enter a long skinny room lined with beds. Most are empty except for one--which is surrounded by a cloth shield for privacy. The nurse stands and gives a little bow. "Our guest requires to see the girl," Mother Superior says. The nurse leads the way.

Pulling back the shield, your throat catches. The girl is pale and, despite the frigid cold of the room, sweats heavy droplets that wet her hair and clothing. Her bosom rises and falls quickly as if she can't catch her breath. The most horrifying thing, however, is her hands and feet. They are tied to the metal bed frame.

"She wouldn't stop flailing and screaming at night. Even with a sedative, she still cried out. It was scaring the other girls," the nurse explains. Drawing up a chair next to the girl, you get permission to examine her.

The Mother Superior Agrees to this.

You may now take the following actions:

- **Check her for bites:** Make a WITS roll now. If you pass, read the text in the box below. If you fail, skip it.

> Looking her body over, you find tiny rat-sized bite marks all along the girl's neck. It seems odd she should have them there. The Mother Superior has no idea how they got there.

- **Hold up a cross to her:** Make a CH roll now. If you fail, the girl begins to flail and scream out as if she were on fire before passing out. You lose 1 Faith. If you pass the CH roll, read the text in the box below.

> The girl writhes and begins to scream. You whisper comforting words of scripture to her and she seems to calm a little. You get her to talk. She speaks of waking up laying on the floor in the abbey. She has no idea how she got there. Last she knew, she was in bed in the dormitory. Thousands of little red eyes stared at her as she lay on the floor before pouncing on her and biting her.

You then ask to be shown to the abbey.

Section 5.0

The Abandoned Abbey

Mother's Light Abbey

1 SQUARE=10FT.

The abbey is a large building at the center of the convent campus. The air seems to grow colder the closer you get, and the building is oddly wrapped in a shroud-like fog while nothing else is.

"This is as far as we are willing to take you." The Mother Superior and Sister Agatha both seem hesitant to even walk on the front steps of the building where you stand.

You nod your understanding and turn toward the building. Could it truly be that this building is inhabited by evil? Is it just a bad infestation of rats, or are the vermin controlled by something far more sinister? Gripping your cross, you enter alone, stepping through the double doors into the chapel.

The Abandoned Abbey is a preconstructed dungeon map. Each room has a number and a corresponding entry here in the book. During gameplay, you will skip the steps for generating rooms, # of doors, and room type. Instead, enter the room and read the text box for the room's entry. Then immediately roll for monsters (including The Chapel). During this dungeon ADD the numerical value of the room to the roll. The closer you get to answers, the more horrific possibilities exist. Once all monsters in a room are defeated, you may then proceed to read the room's other text. Additionally, whenever you move through a doorway that is marked on the map, make a door roll.

Abbey Doorways

(6)	**Unlocked**	Move through freely.
(4–5)	**Stuck**	Must make a ST check to get through. Lose 1 WILL to reroll and try again.
(1–3)	**Locked**	Must make a WI check to get through. Lose 1 WILL to reroll and try again.

	Abbey Monsters				
#	Monster	Max	H-DMG	W-DMG	LF
1	No Monster	–	–	–	–
2	No Monster	–	–	–	–
3	No Monster	–	–	–	–
4	Spider	6	1	1	1
5	Spider Swarm	5	1	1D2	1
6	Mouse	6	1	1D2	2
7	Mouse Swarm	6	1D3	1D2	5
8	Baby Rat	5	1D2	1D2	3
9	Adult Rat	5	1D2	1D3	4
10	Oddly Large Rat	4	1D3	1D3	5
11	Vampire Bat	4	1D3	1D3+1	3
12	Rabid Possum	3	1D3+2	1D3	7
13	Black Cat	3	1D3	1D3+2	4
14	Wolf	2	1D6	1D3+1	10
15	Rat King*	1	1D6	1D6	20

*The Rat King is the boss of this dungeon and will appear in room 9. You may not enter this room until all other rooms are explored.

Room 1: The Chapel

Rows of wooden pews are lined up like silent soldiers, all facing the altar at the east side of the church. Old candelabras adorn the walls and chandeliers hang from the high vaulted ceiling. Despite having only been abandoned for about a week, cobwebs and dust have gathered on everything. If you didn't know it, one might assume the place had been abandoned for decades.

Heading forward to the front of the chapel, you approach the altar. Sitting atop it is an old tattered Bible. Opening it, you begin to read. However, something seems wrong. The passages aren't familiar. The stories seem wrong, skewed somehow, from their original telling. Adam and Eve are demons in the garden. Noah is a bizarre magician who summoned floods to kill all the people of his land. Sarah gets pregnant in her old age but gives birth to a demon child.

Make a WITS check now.

- **If you pass:** You slam the book shut, noticing a strange pentagram insignia on the cover with a crow at the center.
- **If you fail:** You begin to wonder if this is somehow the true bible. Lose 1 Faith.

Room 2: Refectory

This room smells of rot. Multiple long tables with chairs fill the room where nuns once met to eat. As if they left in a hurry without cleaning, plates with bits of food remain. It gives off an awful aroma. The signs of rats also pervade. Nibbled teeth marks in the wooden bowls and the leftover food. Small droppings everywhere.

Covering your mouth, you try not to breathe in any more of the stink than you already have.

Make a ST roll.
- **If you pass:** You rush out of the room.
- **If you fail:** You cough on the smell of droppings taking 1D2 H-DMG.

Room 3: Kitchen

The kitchen is surprisingly tidy. Most
likely the nuns had finished cleaning up
from cooking the last meal before
abandoning the place to the rats and vermin.
However, something strange does catch your
eye. The far counter has a meat carving
knife sitting out. Near it is something red.
Flies buzzing all around.

Taking a chance to look closer at the counter,
you are horrified to see blood drawn out on
the stone in the sign of a pentagram. Bits of
carved flesh, seemingly from human skin,
adorn the corners of the star. It is horrific.
Was some poor soul tortured here? OR did
someone do it to themselves while under the
influence of evil? More and more it seems that
clues point to something far more evil and
sinister being here in the abbey. But what?

Make a WITS roll now.

- **If you pass:** You steel yourself, prepared
  to face something far more sinister than
  you expected.
- **If you fail:** The horror of the bloody
  scene makes your stomach turn and your
  head spin. Lose 1 Health, 2 Willpower,
  and 1 Faith.

Room 4: Larder

Stepping down a few steps into a sunken area, you realize you are in a Larder. This seems to be the coldest room in the whole building. It was probably already designed to keep meats, cheeses, and other food cool, but the country air makes it practically frigid.

The food on the shelves seems to have remained preserved, except for the fact that rats have spoiled it by munching the edges and leaving their droppings in their wake. Moving along a small hallway to one side of the Larder, you sense something that seems off.

Make a WITS roll now.
- **If you pass:** You realize, built into the stone wall, is an old secret door. It was maybe once used to hide valuables, but now it holds something far more horrifying. Bloody implements of torture sit behind the door, and some of the blood looks fresh. Each implement is imprinted with a strange-looking insignia of a pentagram with a crow at the center.
- **If you fail:** You sense nothing new.

Room 5: Hallway

At the back of the Abbey is a tight Hallway that leads to other doorways and rooms.

At the south end of the hallway is a small alcove with a doorway. If you wish to open it, make a door roll now −1.

Once the door is open make a WITs check to investigate. If you pass read the text box below. If you fail, skip the rest of this page. It's just a closet.

Expecting nothing more than a storage closet, you are surprised to see a strange panel in the back of the small space. Pushing on it, you can open it up to reveal a staircase descending into the earth below.

If you follow the tunnel: Entering the dank cold of the underground tunnel, you walk a short way. Pretty soon, you come to another staircase. Climbing up, you open a panel to reveal the hallway of the dormitories. You quickly realize this must have been an escape route for nuns and priests during the inquisition. You quickly return to the abbey.

Room 6: Cloister

This instant you open this door you get a blast of cold air. It seems this room is open to the outside. The outer wall is decorative stone archways that look out on the grounds of the rest of the convent. A small staircase leads down into the grounds. Rain sweeps in, drenching you, and you want nothing more than to get back inside the building.

Once monsters are cleared, you rush back in.

Room 7: Calefactory

This small room has a round stone fireplace in the center with a chimney going up to the middle of the ceiling above. The fire is cold now and you wish there were still some flames there to warm you.

You examine the old ashes of the fireplace, long gone cold. Make a WITS check now. If you pass, read the text box. If you fail, skip it.

You find the remnants of bibles that were burnt here. Who was burning bibles in a nunnery? Who burnt them? If the young girl who was bitten was under the power of a vampire, she might.

Room 8: Preparation Room

This open room has curtains blocking the view from the chapel. It appears to be a simple preparation room with a washbasin to ready yourself for spiritual rites and rituals in the chapel.

The washbasin seems off. The liquid inside of it hardly appears to be water. On closer inspection, you are almost positive that it is blood. You recall Mother Superior claiming it transformed into blood, but is that true? Could it be that someone simply filled it with blood to trick the nuns? Who would do that? More importantly, who's blood is it?

You stare into the blood. Make a CH roll now. If you pass, read the text box. If you fail, skip it.

A vision flashes before you in the reflection of the blood. A nun, someone whom you can't make out the face, walks solemnly through tunnels of some sort of crypt. In her hands, she holds what appears to be a human skull. Coming to a room with an altar, she places the skull inside of a box. You feel it is important to find that box.

Room 9: Mother Superior's Office

You may only enter this room after exploring all others in the Abbey.

This room is large but cozy. Warm chairs and rugs decorate the room. Bookshelves with many books on holy topics line the walls. A large oak desk sits at the center. Somehow, it is less dusty than all the other rooms here.

Unfortunately, the coziness is ruined by the horrific site that clings to the far wall. Seemingly against the laws of nature, a writhing mass of rats, their tails all twisted together, skitters up and down the walls. It moves up toward the ceiling and hangs there. You must now face and kill the Rat King.

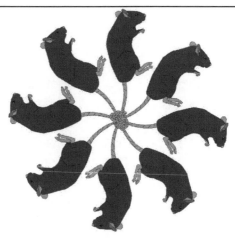

After Killing the Rat King

As you make a final blow against the horrific mass, the fury writhing pile plops down with a sickening wet noise to the ground. Covering your face, you are about to leave when you notice something odd.

The rats sit atop an odd groove in the stone floor. The groove runs under the desk. Stepping forward, you shove the desk with all your might. Make a ST roll. If you fail, spend willpower to reroll. If you have no willpower, you must spend health instead until it is moved.

Once the desk is moved, you reveal a trapdoor beneath. You realize this must be a "Priest Hole" from the inquisition days. It is a place for the priest to hide away from those who might mean him harm.

However, something tells you that this isn't being used to hide a priest anymore. You worry it hides something far more sinister. Opening the trap door, you stare down a dark staircase into a catacomb beneath the abbey.

Section 6.0

The Catacombs

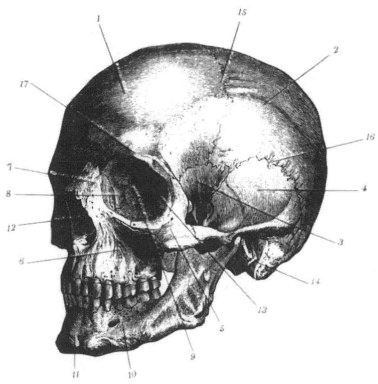

Fig. 1.

Fear grips your throat as you slowly descend into darkness, holding the guttering lantern you found on the desk high for any semblance of light.
You know the answers to the abbey's troubles are hidden down here somewhere, you just don't fancy having to find them. You wonder

how deep these catacombs go. Will you be able to find your way back out?

Catacombs Special Rules:

- Room Type #6 is the final room of the dungeon. You may only find it after every other room type has been found. The boss automatically appears in this room.
- Lost: After completing each room, roll 2D6. If the result is lower than the number of rooms record one "Lost" point. The # of "Lost" points pertains to modifiers on the table below. Then, make a WITS check +/- any modifiers to see if you can remember which way you're going. If you fail, you lose either 1 health, 1 willpower, or 1 faith.

LOST POINTS								
0	2+	4+	6+	8+	10+	12+	14+	16+
−4	−3	−2	−1	0	+1	+2	+3	+4
WITS ROLL MODIFIER								

Dungeon Doorways		
6	**Unlocked**	Move through freely.
4-5	**Stuck**	Must make a ST check to break it open. If you fail, lose 1 WILL to reroll and try again.
2-3	**Locked**	Must make a WI check to pick the lock. If you fail, lose 1 WILL to reroll and try again. If you've found the IRON KEY you don't need to make a check.
1	**Shoddy Door**	The door is shoddy, barely hanging on the hinges. When you move through, the old wooden beam above falls on you. Make a ST check or take 1D2 damage.

Ðungeon Room Types

1	Storage	S	This appears to be a storage room of sorts. It is cluttered with old furniture, barrels, trinkets, and other items that seem of little use. However, the clutter makes battle difficult. +1 on all attacks.
2	Cobwebs	C	This room has thick and heavy cobwebs hanging everywhere, blocking your line of sight. All ranged attacks are made at +1.
3	Tight	T	The ceiling and walls in this room feel too close together, squeezing you in tight. When you enter the room, make a WI check or become claustrophobic, taking 1D3 W-DMG. Then, all melee attacks in this room are made at +1.
4	Rubble	R	Rocks and stones that have fallen make this room difficult to traverse. +1 on all ST and DE rolls in this room.
5	Bodies	B	Dead bodies of long-dead nuns and priests are laid to rest in slots in the walls. Something about looking upon them makes your stomach turn. +1 on all WI and CH rolls in this room.
6	CRYPT	Cr	This is the final room. Turn to section 6.1.

Ðungeon Monsters

#	Monster	Max	H-DMG	W-DMG	LF
1	Rotted Corpse	6	1D3	1D3	2
2	Putrid Rat	6	1D3+1	1D3	5
3	Vampire Bat	4	1D3	1D3+1	3
4	Rabid Possum	3	1D3+2	1D3	7
5	Blood Drinking Corpse	2	1D6	1D3+1	10
6	Unknown Boss*	–	–	–	–

The boss of this dungeon is unknown until you reach the final room and turn to section 6.1. Meanwhile, the blood-drinking corpses, while not vampires themselves, are restless bodies who have somehow been infused with the evil of whatever has been lurking down here. It's almost as if someone has been experimenting on the dead. Therefore, the Blood Drinking Corpses have:

	Bloodletting	Power
Blood Drinking Corpse	1	1

Section 6.1

CRYPT

This room is well lit. Gas lanterns burn along the walls of this large round room. At the center of the room is a stone pedestal and on top of it . . . a wooden box. At the foot of the pedestal lies a woman. Blood oozes from her head and she clutches a book to her chest. Carefully moving closer, you recognize the book. It is a copy of the same one you found on the altar of the chapel. The strange and demented version of The Holy Bible.

You crouch carefully near her to check for breathing when she lets out a scream and sits up. Stumbling back, you recognize her. It is Sister Agatha . . . but she appears much,

much younger. How is it possible, you wonder? Blood drips from two puncture wounds in her neck.

"Sister?" you quietly inquire, your hand instinctively going to your cross when you see her smile and fangs appear.

"Someone took it," she weeps. "Someone took my treasure."

"What treasure?" you ask, your other hand on your weapon.

"The skull," she whispers, nodding toward the wooden box. You look up seeing it is open, and indeed empty.

"What skull?" you wonder out loud.

She smiles again, those fangs glimmering in the firelight from the lanterns. "You took it, didn't you?" she speaks in a hushed voice. "You have it. That's why you came to us. For the skull."

You try to tell her you have no idea what she is speaking of.

However, she won't listen. She lunges at you, fangs barred for a bite.

You must now fight and defeat Sister Agatha

Monster	Max	H-DMG	W-DMG	LF
Sister Agatha	1	1D6	1D6	10
Bloodletting		1D3		
Power		1D2		

Once Agatha is defeated, read the following text box:

Agatha lets out a wild scream, blood oozing from her wounds, and falls into your arms. You watch her visibly start to age. Her hair turns white. Her skin grows wrinkled.

"The skull," she croaks, "Lord VanDrac's skull. I need it. I need it to stay young.

You realize that the skull she speaks of must have once belonged to a vampire. To your horror, she admits to puncturing her neck with the skull's fangs. She had been dying of cancer. Felt weak and old. However, each time she used the skull she had more energy and grew younger. It never lasted. She had to come down again and again to administer the "treatment." The more she did it, however, the more strange things started happening around the abbey. It was like the power of the skull brought all manner of evil to the place.

Mother Superior began to suspect Sister Agatha was up to something but had no proof. Fearing her secret might be found out, she started using an ancient and corrupt version of the bible to bring more horror on the abbey. As her final task, she took a sleeping girl from her bed and placed her in the catacombs where the rats could feast on her blood. This last straw forced them all to move out of the abbey and helped keep her secret for a little longer.

After finally confessing everything, the aging process on Agatha takes hold and she dies. Before your very eyes, she withers to dust and disappears in a gust of wind.

This part of the mystery solved, you return up to the abbey to inform the Mother Superior of what happened.

Section 7.0

Ending the Adventure

Reporting to the Mother Superior, she thanks you for your service. The next day, the abbey seems free and clear of all vermin and rodents. The young girl in the infirmary finally begins recovering. The sun is shining, warming your face as you prepare for the journey back to London, back to headquarters to report. You should feel happy, but you don't. Something is eating at you. This case isn't solved. There are many questions still unanswered.

How had Sister Agatha gotten her hands on such an unholy item as a vampire's skull?

Where had the skull come from?

Who had stolen the skull from her?

Where was the skull now?

What other horrific powers did the skull hold?

Most important of all: Who was Lord VanDrac?

Hammer✠Cross

Character Record Sheet

Name: **Order:**   **Class:**

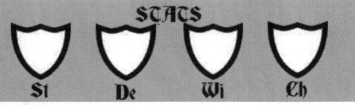

STATS

St   De   Wi   Ch

Proficiency:

WEAPONS

Ranged: **Melee:**

ARMOR   ITEMS

WILL   HEALTH   FAITH   £

Made in the USA
Monee, IL
12 August 2021

75546928R00028